Language on Trial

The Plain English Guide to Legal Writing

Plain English Campaign

Robson Books

This book is dedicated to Chrissie Maher our founder and Director who has dedicated her life to fighting gobbledygook.

First published in Great Britain in 1996 by Robson Books Ltd, Bolsover House, 5-6 Clipstone Street, London W1P 8LE

British Library Cataloguing in Publication Data
A catalogue record for this title is available from the British Library

ISBN 1 86105 006 2

Printed and bound in Great Britain by Hartnolls Ltd., Bodmin, Cornwall

Plain English Campaign
PO Box 3
New Mills
Stockport
SK12 4QP
England
Phone: 01663 744409
Fax: 01663 747038

Contents

Foreword

I am glad to commend Language on Trial.

The law underpins democracy and is part of the birthright of our citizens. It should be clearly expressed and simple to understand.

Yet this is not always so. Law, like most disciplines, has its jargon and its own mystique. This is a barrier to its understanding. A top US lawyer cogently quoted in this book said: "There is probably no single reform that would improve the image of lawyers more than to get them to speak plainly and directly and understandably."

Words are the tools of a lawyer's trade. To use complex, time-hallowed expressions can sometimes give legal certainty. But on other occasions it may just be no more than a comfort and a substitute for clear thought. To speak or write simply demands a clear and confident understanding of the law.

Some great judges are an example and an inspiration. Lord Mansfield, more than two hundred years ago, gave a slave his freedom because "The air of England is too pure for any slave to breathe". In our own century Lord Denning and Lord Reid were masters of crystal clarity. Lord Denning once famously set the scene by saying: "It happened on April 19, 1964. It was bluebell time in Kent." Lord Reid dismissed the argument that public servants should not be sued because they would then be afraid to do their jobs properly by saying, simply, "But my experience leads me to believe that Her Majesty's servants are made of sterner stuff. So I have no hesitation in rejecting this argument." But overall there is much scope for improvement in the language of legal argument, of contracts and of statutes. It is not just lawyers who need to communicate more simply. Business must also do so. We in banking owe it to our customers to let them know clearly what we have to offer, and the terms on which we do business. Communication is a challenge for all of us alike.

I am glad that this year NatWest won the first Plain English "Crystal Clear Bank" award. Now the challenge is for us to keep up the standard and do even better.

This book gives practical, thoughtful and clearly expressed guidance for making the law more accessible through the use of simpler and clearer language. It should provide most food for thought to lawyers, but the principles it sets out are most useful to us all.

Lord Alexander of Weedon QC
Chairman, NatWest Group

Introduction

Plain English Campaign has attacked unclear legal language in the UK for the last fifteen years. We believe that traditional legal language is often inefficient and obscure. We believe that legal documents should and can be written in plainer language. But is this true? Why is legal language the way it is? And how can it be made clearer?

We hope we will answer these questions in this book, and show that writing legal documents in plain English is not just possible, but is a positive advantage for everyone. In chapter 1, we provide a sketch of the forces which have made traditional legal language what it is. In chapter 2 we suggest some reasons why the law needs plain English. Chapter 3 looks at the practicalities of writing law in plain English. We argue that most, though not all, of the peculiarities of traditional legal language are unnecessary and unclear.

Chapter 4 looks at the question of money. And chapter 5 tries to answer the lingering doubts of those who are concerned that plain English law won't have the grandeur of what we have now.

In chapter 6 we get our hands dirty. Here is the fruit of fifteen years' experience – a practical guide to writing in plain English. Plain English Campaign's call for clearer legal language is recognised in the hundreds of legal documents which we have re-written into plain English for many of the biggest companies in the UK and abroad.

We hope that this book will encourage lawyers to use plain English and that it will give other people the information they need to ask their lawyers to do so. Lawyers may sometimes find that we have not gone into all the legal technicalities of a point because the book is also for non-lawyers.

You may wonder what we mean by 'plain English'. It is unfortunate that 'plain' has a range of meanings including 'clear', 'readily understood', 'simple', 'undecorated', 'ugly' and 'unsophisticated'. We can define plain English as 'writing which communicates to the reader as clearly as possible'. Not all plain English documents will be equally easy to understand – it depends on the complexity of the subject matter. Plain English is not a substandard version of English. It is not 'Peter and Jane'. It is not boring or ugly. Plain English can blossom into metaphor, provided it's still clear.

Chrissie Maher OBE MA

Founder and Director
Plain English Campaign

Footnotes for each chapter are at the end of that chapter. Full details of the books referred to are in 'Further Reading' on page 88.

Chapter 1

...all the residue unexpired...

Why is legal language as it is?

'But habit is a great deadener.'
Samuel Beckett, *Waiting for Godot*

'Again, Mr Micawber had a relish in this formal piling up of words, which, however ludicrously displayed in his case, was, I must say, not at all peculiar to him. I have observed it, in the course of my life, in numbers of men. It seems to me to be a general rule. In the taking of legal oaths, for instance, deponents seem to enjoy themselves mightily when they come to several good words in succession, for the expression of one idea; as, that they utterly detest, abominate, and abjure, or so forth; and the old anathemas were made relishing on the same principle. We talk about the tyranny of words, but we like to tyrannise over them too; we are fond of having a large superfluous establishment of words to wait upon us on great occasions; we think it looks important and sounds well. As we are not particular about the meaning of our liveries on state occasions, if they be but fine and numerous enough, so the meaning and necessity of our words is a secondary consideration, if there be but a great parade of them. And as individuals get into trouble by making too great a show of liveries, or as slaves when they are too numerous rise against their masters, so I think I could mention a nation that has got into many great difficulties, and will get into many greater, from maintaining too large a retine of words.'

Charles Dickens, *David Copperfield*

Most people recognise legal language when they see it. Here's a real example, drafted by a lawyer for his client:

THIS DEED OF DECLARATION OF TRUST is made the eighteenth day of August One Thousand Nine Hundred and Ninety Two BETWEEN LAURA SMITH of The Wood Mill Hamden Derbyshire (hereinafter called "Miss Smith") of the one part and STEPHEN BREAKHOUSE of The Wood Mill Hamden aforesaid (hereinafter called "Mr Breakhouse") of the other part

WHEREAS:-

1. By an assignment of even date herewith but executed before this Deed and made between Robert Mark Paine and Janet Louise Paine of the one part and Miss Smith of the other part the leasehold property known as The Wood Mill Hamden aforesaid was assigned to Miss Smith for all the residue unexpired of a term of Nine hundred and ninety years from the 6th June 1980 created by an Underlease dated 6th June 1980 more particularly described in the said Assignment for her own use and benefit absolutely

2. By a Legal Charge of even date herewith and also executed before this Deed Miss Smith charged the property with payment to SaveFast Home Loans Limited as chargee for the sum of Thirty nine thousand pounds borrowed by Miss Smith from SaveFast Home Loans Limited with interest thereon at the rate and by the instalments and subject to the terms of conditions therein set forth

3. Miss Smith wishes to give to Mr Breakhouse an undivided equal share of and in her interest in The Wood Mill

It is obviously a kind of English. But it is also obviously not everyday English. What is it that sets legal language apart? And why is it the way it is?

What is so odd about legal language?

Legal language has a number of characteristics. Few of these are unique to lawyers, but together they produce the distinctive flavour of writing like the piece above. Here are some of the characteristics.

Hundreds of uncommon words and phrases. These include:

- Latin words, like *inter alia* ('among others') and *pro rata* ('in proportion');

- words no longer in everyday use, like 'herein' and 'aforesaid';

- words that have never been in everyday use (in English), like 'lien' and 'novation'; and

- everyday words that have special meanings for lawyers, like 'action' (a law suit) and 'instrument' (a legal document).

Wordiness

Legal language tends to use too many words. The law is littered with phrases which are saying the same thing twice ('null and void') or three times ('rest, residue and remainder'). Lawyers also add unnecessary words and phrases. (See chapter 3 for a good example.)

Long sentences

Lawyers tend to write long sentences.

Punctuation

Lawyers frequently miss out punctuation completely or use it wrongly.

Passive verbs

Lawyers prefer passive verbs to active verbs. (See chapter 6 for an explanation of what we mean by 'active' and 'passive'.)

Formality

Legal language tends to be unnecessarily formal. In fact it needs to be no more formal than any other kind of modern business writing.

Impersonality

The law is about people. It rarely seems as if it is.

Why is legal language like this?

We want to identify three major causes for the peculiar state of legal language.

1 An exclusive profession

When people nowadays say that lawyers speak a different language they are exaggerating. But it hasn't always been an exaggeration. After the Norman invasion in 1066, the languages of England became English, French and, for the well-educated, Latin.

For a time, among the upper classes at least, people commonly spoke both French and English. But, within 200 years of the Normans' arrival, French was definitely in decline. 250 years after that, it was, with one exception, dead.

The exception, you will not be surprised to learn, was the law. Lawyers continued to mix a peculiar version of French into their writing for hundreds of years. A law was passed in 1731 requiring that lawyers must write:

> in the *English* tongue and language only, and not in *Latin* or *French* or any other tongue or language whatsoever.[1]

By then, French in English law was already dying out. It remains now only in a collection of French words which have become part of the English language (for example, 'sentence', 'tort' and 'fee simple'). But why did the French survive so long?

It is revealing, we think, that lawyers began to use *more* French in the law just when the general public (and particularly the lower classes) were speaking *less* French. Historians still argue over the hazy mechanics of these changes, but, as David Mellinkoff, American expert on legal language, puts it:

> What better way of preserving a professional monopoly than by locking up your trade secrets in the safe of an unknown tongue?

Mellinkoff is repeating a complaint that echoes down the centuries. The general public have long believed that the language of the law is designed to keep them in the dark and the lawyers in the money.

In the past, lawyers have said precisely that. In 1658, William Style thought that the law which had been published in English:

hath only occasioned the making of unquiet spirits contentiously knowing, and more apt to offend others, than to defend themselves.

Historically, lawyers and law-makers have deliberately excluded the public from the law by the use of unclear legal language.

The lawyers' and law-makers' reasons for this ranged from genuine concern that knowledge of the law would confuse rather than inform those with no legal education, to a simple desire to keep the workers quiet.

Few lawyers now would admit to deliberately trying to exclude the public. Many of them honestly believe that they cannot make the law any clearer for lay people. (We'll be looking at that belief throughout this book.)

But three essential points remain.

- The language of the law has partly been shaped by lawyers wishing to baffle the public. Even if the desire is gone, legal language continues to hide the law from the people it controls and protects.

- Legal language's difference from everyday speech identifies the writer as a lawyer. Indeed, for some people, legal language is the mark of a 'proper' lawyer. Faced with a lump of difficult legalese, lay people think: 'I can't understand a word. This must be the work of an expert.'

- Just as legal language is part of the lay person's vision of what a lawyer is, so it is part of what a lawyer thinks a lawyer is. As in all professions with their own languages, legal language helps lawyers to feel they belong. (Which means, of course, that they fear professional ridicule if they change to plain English.)

In other words, **legal language is a different language in order to show everyone who reads it that lawyers are different.** It is the badge of their profession. At the same time, because legal language baffles the lay person, it contributes to the difference which it marks. For hundreds of years, incomprehensible legal language has been part of the legal profession's attempts to maintain its monopoly of understanding.

2 Language under siege

Legal language is a language under siege. The language we speak every day can sometimes be loose and careless. Legal language cannot afford to be either.

If someone fails to put down accurately what they mean to say, a lawyer may very well find the gap and exploit it.

Just as a piece of metal twists under a heavy weight, so this pressure has shaped and continues to shape legal language. Some of the results of this pressure are useful.

You might say to a friend: 'You're welcome to stay in my house. But you'll have to pay £25 a week to help cover the bills.' But if you were a landlord, you would expect to sign a long agreement with your tenant just in case your tenant decided to hold barbecues in the sitting room or organise small rock concerts in the middle of the night. Legal language must 'stand up in court'. It must not be possible to misunderstand it, deliberately or accidentally.

On the other hand, the pressure on legal language also produces unnecessary exactness and comprehensiveness. This is what we call 'belt and braces' legal language: for fear of not saying the right thing, the writer says it twice or more.

Look at the part of a document which we put at the beginning of the chapter. The lawyer will write 'The Wood Mill Hamden aforesaid' over and over again, even though, after saying 'The Wood Mill Hamden Derbyshire' in the first sentence, you could hardly mean a different 'Wood Mill'. (The document seems to recognise this in point 3, where it just says 'The Wood Mill'.)

Obviously, the writer needs to make it clear which 'Wood Mill' they mean: the intention is sensible. It's just that, being naturally cautious, the writer has gone over the top.

The pressure on legal language is caused by the way in which the courts interpret legal language. What Lord Denning has said about writing laws could, perhaps, apply to legal language generally:

> It is because the judges have not felt it right to fill in the gaps and have given a literal interpretation for many years that the draughtsman has felt that he has to try and think of every conceivable thing and put it in as far as he can so that even the person unwilling to understand will follow it. I think the rules of interpretation which the judges have applied have been one of the primary causes why draughtsmen have felt that they must have a system of over-detailed, over-long sentences, and obscurity. [2]

This isn't the place to discuss the arguments about legal interpretation. But legal language today has certainly been shaped by a tradition of sometimes excessively literal interpretation. (By 'literal interpretation' we mean interpreting a document mostly by the words themselves and not in the light of the intention of those words, their context, other relevant laws and so on.) So, **legal language has been shaped by the constant threat of attack in court.**

3 Inertia

Most people continue doing things in the same way until they have a good reason to change. The way English law works strengthens this tendency.

First of all, leading on from what we have just said about language under siege, fear of attack also leads to fear of change. If a particular wording has been attacked in court and survived, then it is better to repeat it than risk trying new language.

Second, a large part of British law is 'precedent'. That is, if a court has decided something in the past, you can use that decision to argue that the court should make the same decision now.

Third, on a more practical level, most legal writing is based on standard documents. It is fairly rare for a solicitor to write a legal document from scratch. So the style of yesterday becomes the style of today.

Most languages, used in everyday situations, evolve to cope with changes in the outside world. Language is also continuously being streamlined by being used every day. If it takes a long time to say 'designing and typesetting publications on a personal computer', we learn to say 'desktop publishing' (or, for the whiz kids, 'DTP').

All languages bear the traces of their pasts, but languages are continuously modified by the way they are used today. With legal language, the balance between these two forces is quite different. For the reasons that we have suggested above, legal language has always developed with a greater regard for its past than has ordinary language. The result is the legal language we have now – a language full of relics from a past which everyday English has long left behind. Three examples:

1 'Aforesaid', 'herein', 'hereby', 'said' (as in 'the said cottage'), 'thereon', 'thereto', 'witnesseth' and so on were all parts of everyday English once (in the Middle Ages or earlier). They are now rarely used outside the law and other kinds of official language.

2 Look at the piece of legal language we quoted at the beginning of the chapter. Why does it say 'residue unexpired' and 'The Wood Mill Hamden aforesaid'? In English, with very few exceptions, the adjective sits in front of the noun: 'red balloon', 'small child' *not* 'balloon red', 'child small'. In normal English, if we were going to use these words at all, we would say 'unexpired residue' and 'the aforesaid Wood Mill, Hamden'.

The reason for this strange characteristic of legal language is simple: in French the adjective usually sits *after* the noun. (And in Latin, the adjective can be placed before or after.) As we've already said, lawyers clung (and are still clinging) to their French and Latin long after the rest of the country was using only English. This quirk is another residue (unexpired) of those languages.

3 Perhaps the most bizarre case of all is the law's attitude to punctuation. The Greeks and Romans often didn't use punctuation at all. When they did, it was a messy business, with no set rules. Punctuation was used just to tell someone how to read something aloud. The job of punctuation has changed considerably since then. Since the Middle Ages, punctuation, like spelling, has gradually been fixed by rules. In modern English, punctuation is a reliable guide to interpreting a series of words, as well as to correct stress and intonation when reading aloud.

The law has, predictably, been cautious about relying on punctuation. Supported by the myth that Acts of Parliament were not punctuated in the past, judges for a long time disregarded punctuation when interpreting laws.[3]

Very few statute lawyers or judges really support this any more.

The late Reed Dickerson, probably the greatest recent expert on legal writing in the USA, said that punctuation is 'a tool that the draughtsman can ill afford to neglect'[4]. One of the leading British statute draughtsmen says 'The truth is that punctuation in an Act should be regarded the way it is in any other text, as an aid to understanding.'[5]

But the message hasn't reached the legal profession generally. Look at the piece of legal language we quoted at the beginning. It's pretty clear where the full stops ought to go. Why leave them out?

In short, **legal language is wedded to the past and afraid of the future.**

But there is another way of looking at the peculiarities of legal language. Looking at a language so loaded with history, we may feel nostalgic regret, rather than irritation. If legal language is such a great part of the tradition of the law, do we *really* need plain English? We will begin to answer this question in the next chapter.

---

1 *Records in English*, 1731, quoted in David Mellinkoff, *The Language of the law*, pages 133-4.

2 The Renton Report: *The Preparation of Legislation*, paragraph 19.1, quoted in Sir Rupert Cross, *Statutory Interpretation*, page 195.

3 The 'myth' is conclusively demolished in David Mellinkoff, *The Language of the Law*, pages 157-164.

4 Reed Dickerson, *The Fundamentals of Legal Drafting*, page 188.

5 Francis Bennion, *Statute Law*, page 57.

Chapter 2

...the Rule of Lottery...

Do we need plain English in the law?

> 'I said there was a society of men among us, bred up
> from their youth in the art of proving by words multiplied
> for the purpose, that white is black, and black is white,
> according as they are paid... It is likewise to be observed
> that this society hath a peculiar cant and jargon of their
> own, that no other mortal can understand, and wherein
> all their laws are written, which they take special care to
> multiply; whereby they have wholly confounded the very
> essence of truth and falsehood, of right and wrong.'

Jonathan Swift, *Gulliver's Travels*

Gulliver's attack on legal gobbledygook is the strongest call
for clearer legal language we have seen. But it doesn't win
the argument. For one thing, it's over 250 years old. For
another, it becomes clear to the reader at the end of
Gulliver's Travels that Gulliver is mad.

Is the situation as bad now? Sadly, Gulliver might almost have
been talking yesterday. Language proving that 'white is black,
and black is white' is still all too often just what lawyers
write.

Listen to the US Court of Appeals Judge, Ruggero J Aldisert:

> Brief writing runs from abysmal to mediocre. About 10
> per cent of the briefs I read are briefs that really show
> professional skill at written communications.[1]

(Note for non-lawyers: a brief, in America, is a document
written by a lawyer presenting his or her case to a court.)
There have always been lawyers who write clearly and well.

And some lawyers have made a great deal of progress towards plain English in the last twenty years. But there is still a long way to go. The need for plain English is as great as it was in Gulliver's time, for three reasons: moral, legal and practical.

Moral

At its worst, legal language hurts people. Gobbledygook makes people think that there is something wrong with them when they fail to understand. It means that they do not know their rights and do not get the help they desperately need. It leaves them confused, irritated and humiliated.

Very often, people encounter the law when they are most vulnerable: after the death of someone they love; when a marriage collapses; or when they are arrested. And all too often, it is the people who most need protection who are least able to understand the law.

The Adult Literacy and Basic Skills Unit (ALBSU) recently carried out a survey of the reading abilities of adults in the UK. ALBSU measures people's reading by testing them with a variety of everyday reading and writing tasks. 16% of the people surveyed (about one person in six) were below ALBSU level 1. ALBSU considers that level 1 is the lowest acceptable level of reading and writing ability.

To give you a clearer idea of what this means, to reach level 1 you need to be able to:

- read and understand a short feature in a newspaper or magazine;

- use reference material like Yellow Pages or a dictionary to get simple information;

- deal with an application form for a job; and

- write formal letters, reports or notes, giving up to four separate ideas.

And 16% of the people surveyed in the UK over the age of 16 could not do these things. [2]

As Lord Simon of Glaisdale said to the Statute Law Society, speaking about British statutes:

> A society whose regulations are incomprehensible lives with the Rule of Lottery, not of Law. [3]

Whether you are signing a contract, communicating with your solicitor, making a will or looking into some particular legal problem, the ability to understand the law is a basic right and a basic need. Early in the seventeenth century, although he was talking about translating the law from French into English, one of the greatest writers of English law, Sir Edward Coke, made the crucial point:

> I cannot conjecture that the general communication of these laws into the English tongue can work any inconvenience, but introduce great profit, seeing that *Ignorantia juris non excusat*, Ignorance of the law excuseth not. [4]

This principle – that it is no defence to claim you didn't know what you were doing was illegal – is still part of British law today. But if people cannot understand the legal documents which they must live by, you have to ask quite what we mean by a 'democratic society'.

There is a more subtle moral argument about legal language too. As several experts on legal writing have argued, legal writing makes its subject less human. As we said in Chapter 1, the law is about real people in real situations. In its efforts, perhaps, to preserve 'the majesty of the law', legal language sounds more like the voice of a machine, talking about impersonal processes.

Richard Lanham, author of a highly regarded guide to writing well, writes:

> Human beings, we need to remind ourselves here, are social beings.... We become uneasy if, for extended periods of time, we neither hear nor see other people. We feel uneasy with the Official Style for the same reason. It has no human voice, no face, no personality behind it. It creates no society, encourages no social conversation. We feel that it is *unreal*. [5]

Perhaps, then, the impersonal nature of the law's voice makes the law less humane. [6]

Throughout its history, legal gobbledygook, whether deliberately or not, has excluded those without a legal education from laws which affect them. It does not need to be like this. It should not be like this.

Legal

In the past, British courts have had little sympathy with people who have signed a contract without fully understanding it.

This is understandable. If the courts were continually overturning contracts, the business world would fall apart, unable to do business with confidence. So, once you had signed it, a contract was sacred, however small the print or unclear the language. (There are some exceptions to this, but none are really concerned with clear English.) [7]

But today lawyers around the English-speaking world are being coaxed into changing their writing. Over the last twenty years, US states, the European Commission and, to a lesser extent, the UK government have produced laws requiring that contracts be intelligible. And it is likely that the legal pressure on lawyers to write plain English is going to increase.

In the US, eight states have laws insisting on plain English in consumer contracts in general and 36 states have laws just covering insurance policies.

The first of the eight general laws requires that every consumer contract for a deal of less than $50,000 be:

● written in a clear and coherent manner using words with common and everyday meanings; and

● appropriately divided and captioned by its various sections.

If a consumer can prove that they have actually lost money because of an unclear contract, they can claim damages but the contract still holds. And the Attorney General of the state can take a business to court if he or she believes that it is breaking the plain English law.

Only two consumers have taken cases to court about unclear contracts. Instead, the law has worked by encouraging change. Once it was introduced, there were, in the (not totally plain) words of one commentary on New York's laws:

large-scale compliance efforts by major industries resulting in introduction of many new forms, both by . . industries and form-preparing firms.

In Australia, the Trade Practices Commission, the Insurance and Superannuation Commission and other government departments are all putting pressure on businesses to produce contracts in clear English. And in court, in both New Zealand and Australia, judges have penalized companies which have produced incomprehensible documents.

In Britain, the Unfair Contract Terms Act of 1977 offers little real protection against unclear English. If the Act defines part of a contract as unfair, the contract is then invalid whether it is in plain language or not. A lawyer could argue that a contract term was unfair because it was incomprehensible, but this rather indirect threat is unlikely to make a company rewrite its contracts.

In 1984, the National Consumer Council suggested a plain language law for the UK. In December 1992, Gyles Brandreth MP put forward a plain English bill in Parliament. It was not successful.

In reality, however, the European Commission has overtaken the British Parliament on this issue. Article 5 of the EC Unfair Contract Terms Directive says:

> In the case of contracts where all or certain terms offered to the consumer are in writing, these terms must always be drafted in plain, intelligible language. Where there is doubt about the meaning of a term, the interpretation most favourable to the consumer shall prevail.

The Department of Trade and Industry has now implemented the Directive with its Unfair Terms in Consumer Contracts Regulations, which became law on 1 July 1995.

In the UK, in contracts at least, plain English is as much a legal as a moral necessity.

Practical

Many people, lawyers and non-lawyers alike, are prepared to accept that, morally and legally, plain English is a good idea. But there are practical questions. Plain English does not work in the law, they say. It is not precise enough. The law in plain English loses all its grandeur. We don't have time to write in plain English. It will cost us too much money. You can't make a complex subject simple. And so on.

These are not unreasonable complaints. As we have already said, the law makes special demands of language. Perhaps the law requires a special kind of language.

Over the next three chapters, we will show not only that plain English works, but that it is very much needed.

We will argue that plain English:

- can do the job of traditional legal language (chapter 3);

- saves money (chapter 4); and

- needn't be dull and unimpressive (chapter 5).

And we will argue that unclear legal language:

- is largely unnecessary and sometimes dangerously misleading (chapter 3);

- is costly and inefficient (chapter 4); and

- has damaged the image of the law (chapter 5).

These are the practical reasons for making the language of the law plain language.

---

1 Charlotte Low Allen, 'Skilled legal writing becomes exceptional', *Insight on the news*, Dec 25 1989 – Jan 1990, page 50.

2 For more information, see *Making it happen: Improving Basic Skills for the 21st Century*, ALBSU, 1994.

3 Lord Simon of Glaisdale, 'The Renton Report – Ten Years On', page 133.

4 Sir Edward Coke, *Commentary upon Littleton* xxxviii-xxxix (Butler, 19th ed 1832).

5 Richard Lanham, *Revising Prose*, page 66

6 See Steven Stark, 'Why Lawyers Can't Write' in *Harvard Law Review*, Vol 97 pages 1389-93 for a moving and powerful argument that this is the case.

7 See Richard Thomas, *Plain words for Consumers* , pages 17-24 for a discussion of the legal situation.

Chapter 3

...unambiguous, precise, comprehensive and largely conventional...

Can the law survive without traditional legal language?

> 'Legal drafting must therefore be unambiguous, precise, comprehensive and largely conventional. If it is readily intelligible, so much the better; but it is far more important that it should yield its meaning accurately than it should yield it on first reading, and the legal draughtsman cannot afford to give much attention, if any, to euphony [pleasant sound] or literary elegance.'
>
> Sir Bruce Fraser, *The Complete Plain Words*

Can the language of the law be made plain? Bruce Fraser's exception for legal language in one of the plain English movement's founding documents continues to haunt the fight for plain English.

Most of the time legal gobbledygook is not questioned. But when it is, the lawyer's main defence remains essentially the same. Yes, legal gobbledygook is difficult to understand, but (bowing to Sir Bruce) 'it is far more important that it should yield its meaning accurately than it should yield it on first reading'. Legal language is able to communicate complex ideas accurately. Plain English just wouldn't be up to it.

Where Sir Bruce got it wrong

This is a standard piece of legal language from an insurance contract:

The due observance and fulfilment of the terms so far as

they relate to anything to be done or complied with by the Insured and the truth of the statements and answers in the Proposal shall be conditions precedent to any liability of the Company to make any payment under this policy.

It is also, as you will realise if you've deciphered it, absolutely crucial. Essentially, it tells the person who has the policy that if they don't follow the terms of the policy or if they have lied on the form they've filled in (the 'Proposal'), the company can refuse to give them any money.

Is the legal language necessary to say this accurately?

No.

Let's take this piece of writing apart.

The main point that will puzzle the lay person reading this is the word 'precedent'. As a noun, 'precedent' is a reasonably well-known word. As an adjective, it fools most people. As a lawyer would recognise, it's there because it's part of the common legal jargon 'conditions precedent'. According to L B Curzon's *Dictionary of Law*, a condition precedent is something which must happen before you can give someone a legal right. Here, however, 'conditions precedent' really has no technical meaning which we cannot communicate in ordinary language. The essence of the 'condition precedent' is that something can happen **only if** something else **has** happened. So we'll re-write the sentence to say that:

> There will be liability of the Company to make any payment under this Policy **only if** there **has** been the due observance and fulfilment of the terms so far as they relate to anything to be done or complied with by the Insured and the statements and answers in the Proposal **are** true.

Of course, we're not thinking of leaving it like that. We just want to show that 'conditions precedent' is an unnecessary phrase. If the insurance company had thought about it, they could have stopped puzzling more or less every lay person who read their policy. As it was, very few of their customers would understand what a 'condition precedent' was.

Another common characteristic of legal language is that it tends to be impersonal. This makes it both less friendly and more difficult to understand. It's easier to understand 'you' and 'we' than 'the Insured' and 'the Company' because we say and hear 'you' and 'we' every day. (Of course, you can't use 'you' and 'we' in all kinds of legal writing.) We know much more quickly who 'you' and 'we' refer to so our sentence now reads:

> There will be liability for **us** to make any payment under this Policy only if there has been the due observance and fulfilment of the terms so far as they relate to anything to be done or complied with by **you** and the statements and answers in **your** Proposal are true.

Bad official writing in general tends to twist around the normal word order of sentences. Let's rearrange this sentence like this:

> **We will be liable** to make any payment under this Policy only if **you have duly observed and fulfilled** the terms so far as they relate to anything to be done or complied with by you and the statements and answers in your Proposal are true.

We've made nouns back into verbs, so that 'there has been the due observance' becomes 'you have duly observed'. Sentences written like this are generally easier to understand.

The important point here is that we've been able to get rid of these two characteristics of legal language without losing any of the legal meaning. All we've done is make the sentence clearer – but only slightly.

So we've got rid of 'conditions precedent' and rearranged the sentence to make it easier to read. Let's have another look at it.

Another characteristic of legal language is its obsessive desire to be, as Sir Bruce said, 'unambiguous, precise, [and] comprehensive'. Of course, lawyers need to write legal language that meets these criteria. But a lot of the time this leads to attempts at precision and comprehensiveness that deliver nothing of the sort. In fact, the words and phrases used are merely 'conventional'.

What does 'if you have duly observed and fulfilled the terms so far as they relate to anything to be done or complied with by you' mean?

Does 'duly observed and fulfilled the terms' mean anything more than 'kept to the terms'? Surely if you've duly observed the terms of an insurance policy, you've also fulfilled the terms of an insurance policy? In the same way, does 'to be done or complied with by you' mean anything more than 'to be complied with by you'? This is 'belt and braces' legal thinking.

Worse still, ask yourself 'Would a court expect you to observe and fulfil those terms of an insurance policy which did not relate to anything to be done or complied with by you?' This is like saying:

You must do those things which you must do (but you don't need to worry about the things which don't apply to you.)

It's hogwash.

Version four:

We will be liable to make any payment under this Policy only **if you have kept to the terms of the Policy** and the statements and answers in your Proposal are true.

This is 32 words long, compared to the original's 52 words. One word remains which will puzzle too many lay people – liable. Can we get rid of it? We need to ask, 'What is the essential message here?' It is that:

> If you haven't done these two things, we do not have to pay you any money.

If we put this idea back into our sentence, and use layout to make the sentence easier to read, we end up with:

> We will only make a payment under this Policy if:

- you have kept to the terms of the Policy; and
- the statements and answers in your Proposal are true.

This, we think, communicates the essentials of the original accurately and clearly.

Lawyers we have spoken to have raised one major objection. Ask yourself this question.

> If I have kept to the terms of the Policy and the statements and answers in my Proposal are true, do I then have an automatic right to a payment under my Policy?

The lawyers' worry is that by removing the word 'liable' we risk saying that:

> We will make a payment under this Policy, *whether your claim is valid or not* if:

- you have kept to the terms of the Policy; and
- the statements and answers in your Proposal are true.

Which, of course, would destroy the insurance company.

But. . .

This sentence is only one of the terms of an insurance policy. Other terms say that you can only get money out of the insurance company if your carpets, car or children really have been stolen, damaged or covered in paint. In its context, this term is clear. And it must be interpreted in its context, because the term says 'We will only make a payment **under this Policy** if . . .'.

The plain English version survives. Not only can plain English do the job of legal language, it does it in 20 words fewer than the insurance company's version. Plain English law is usually, but not always, shorter than the traditional legal version because, as we've just seen, when we look at a piece of traditional legal language, we can throw a lot of it into the bin.

This is only a small part of an insurance contract. But it is not a bad demonstration of how we can simplify legal language. Looking at what we have just done, we can now list the elements that made the original version difficult to understand.

1 An unnecessary technical term - 'condition precedent'.

2 An impersonal style.

3 Twisted word order.

4 Needless repetition and elaboration.

5 Unhelpful layout.

6 One technical term which may be slightly more justifiable (and more generally understood) – 'liable'.

All of these, with the possible exception of 6, are quite unnecessary to the legal working of this part of an insurance contract.

Slaying more monsters

As 2, 3, 4 and 5 suggest, many of the peculiarities of legal language are features of 'official writing' generally.
These include:

● sentences that go on and on;

● passive verbs where you could use active ones;

● confusing word order;

● fancy words where you could use everyday ones;

● a lack of planning; and

● a message that is not clearly thought out.

In short, a lot of what is wrong with legal writing is that it is bad writing and the law will survive without that. (We'll go through a complete course of first aid for sick writing in chapter 6.)

Many of the words and phrases characteristic of legal language tend, like 'condition precedent', to be unnecessary. As we discussed in chapter 1, the law, naturally enough, tends to look to the past for reassurance. If lawyers have used a word or phrase for the last 100 or 500 or 1000 years, then surely it must be effective to have survived so long. Unfortunately, this is rarely the case.

It is up to lawyers to clear their working vocabulary of encrusted rubbish and find clearer alternatives. Richard Wydick, an American expert on clear legal language, writes;

> This is not as simple as it sounds. Lawyers are busy, cautious people, and they cannot afford to make mistakes. The old, redundant phrase has worked in the past; a new one may somehow raise a question. To

check it in the law library will take time, and time is the lawyer's most precious commodity. But remember – once you slay one of these old monsters, it will stay dead for the rest of your legal career. If your memory is short, keep a card file of slain redundancies. Such trophies distinguish a lawyer from a scrivener.[1]

To show how much legal vocabulary is unnecessary (and, if you're a lawyer, to give you a head start with that card file), here are some examples of classic legal verbiage.

Aforesaid. Aforesaid's 'purpose is to refer to something that has been said, and its chief vice is that you can't be sure what it refers to'. (David Mellinkoff)

If a lawyer writes 'the field aforesaid' it can have two possible effects.

- There is only one field in the document so far, in which case 'aforesaid' is unnecessary.

- There is more than one field, in which case 'aforesaid' fails to say which one the lawyer means.

Using 'aforesaid', and its big sister 'aforementioned', is a pointless habit which at best wastes space and at worst hides unclear thinking. Exactly the same argument is true for that other regular feature of legal gobbledygook – 'said', as in 'the said field'.

Indeed, we can include in the same group a ragbag of words left over from the Middle Ages – 'herein', 'hereinafter', 'hereafter' and so on – all of which litter legal language and all of which are dangerously vague. Mellinkoff points out an extraordinary case in 1950-51 in California which hinged on the meaning of 'Except as herein expressly provided'. The court at the first trial decided that 'herein' meant 'in this whole statute'. (Note for non-lawyers: a statute is a complete law, like, say, the Dangerous Dogs Act 1990.) The appeal decided that herein meant 'in this section'. Then four Supreme Court judges swung back with 'in this whole statute'. In all, enough public money to build a small hospital was wasted.

Last will and testament You may think we are mean to strike out at this old favourite. But it is the best known example of an absurd legal habit which we have already seen at the start of the chapter: needless repetition.

'Will' and 'testament' mean exactly the same thing. 'Will' is from Old English and 'testament' is its Latin equivalent. 'Last' comes from the time when your will was your last dying words. Now that many people go through several wills before they die, some lawyers take last to mean most recent. In either case, it is unnecessary. After all, no one writes a 'second-to-last will and testament'. 'Last' can and has caused confusion after someone has died. Instead of 'Last will and testament', use 'will'.

Whether you are a lawyer or not, you have probably encountered some of the following: 'null and void'; 'mind and memory'; 'to have and to hold'; 'fit and proper'; 'force and effect'; 'give, devise and bequeath'; 'rest, residue and remainder'; 'due and payable'; and 'goods and chattels'. [2]

And if you haven't, try this (the bold type is ours):

1. By an assignment of even date herewith but executed before this Deed and made between Robert Mark Paine and Janet Louise Paine of the one part And Miss Smith of the other part the leasehold property known as The Wood Mill Hamden aforesaid was assigned to Miss Smith for all the **residue unexpired** of a term of Nine hundred and ninety years from the 6th June 1980 created by an Underlease dated 6th June 1980 more particularly described in the said Assignment for her own use and benefit absolutely.

What does 'residue unexpired' mean? What other kind of residue can you have? And so on.

The limits of plain English

The myth about legal gobbledygook is that it is a vital part of the lawyer's art and that it has abilities in communication which ordinary language lacks. The reality is that plain legal language works because the vast majority of what makes legal language difficult to understand is not necessary to the law – it only survives because of habit, fear of mistakes and ignorance.

Having said that, we need to make clear the limits of plain English in the law. We don't want to give the impression (particularly with the insurance example) that re-writing in plain English is like some crude factory process. You can't put a piece of impenetrable legal writing in at one end of a machine and wait for it to be spat out, crystal clear, at the other end.

Plain English legal writing, like all writing, takes place in a context. For legal writing, the context includes the client's wishes, the rest of the document, and the rules of law.

Writing a legal document in plain English is not just about writing. A legal document is written to reliably bring about a particular situation. Lawyers must think through the essentials of that situation and find the clearest language which will accurately bring it about. Often, 'translating' a document into plain English means re-thinking its aims too.

You can't make a complex subject simple. Here, again, the insurance example may be misleading. It is, after all, a pretty simple part of an insurance contract. Enormously complicated tax laws cannot be made as clear as the Green Cross Code: the ease of understanding of a piece of writing will be limited by the complexity of its content.

But this doesn't let legal writers off the hook. All too often they go from saying that the law is a complex subject (it is) to writing in a style that is *unnecessarily* complicated. It should be obvious that the more difficult the content is to understand, the harder lawyers should work to express it clearly.

We are not trying to say that plain English suddenly makes the law easy to understand. But it makes it *easier* to understand. Legal writers tend to underestimate how much they can do to clarify complex information.

Legal language will never be the same as everyday English. As we discussed in chapter 1, legal language has been shaped by its environment and uses. Much of what we have now is unnecessary and unclear. But a part is not.

Lawyers need to express themselves more carefully than people in everyday situations. The lawyer can't afford loopholes or confusion. To take a very simple example from the document in chapter 1, although it is ridiculous to write 'The Wood Mill Hamden aforesaid' throughout the document, the lawyer needs to make absolutely clear somewhere in the document that the house he or she is talking about is 'The Wood Mill, Hamden, Derbyshire'. In everyday English, we might just write 'The Wood Mill' and expect our readers to know which house we were referring to. But the lawyer cannot take that risk. This pressure on legal language inevitably means it will not be the same as everyday English. All we are saying is that legal language doesn't need to be as different as most lawyers think.

Also, some of the words lawyers use do have special legal meanings – 'terms of art'. A term of art is a word or phrase which has an established meaning in the law because it has been used over the years in a fairly fixed way. A term of art doesn't necessarily have a narrowly defined meaning, but it must have a reasonably reliable range of meanings. 'Plaintiff', 'hearsay', 'surrender (a lease)' are all terms of art. Over the years they have gained specific legal meanings. They cover in one or a few words a complex idea with a particular history.

But here too, lawyers tend to exaggerate the problem in order to justify bad legal writing. As we saw with 'condition precedent', a supposedly vital 'term of art' can turn out to be an unnecessary complication. Bryan Garner, an American expert, estimates that there are no more than 50 essential words. Another expert, Robert W Benson, says: 'Surely, the list does not exceed 100 terms'.[3]

Even with those 100, lawyers can still help their readers to understand. This depends on what they are writing and for whom. If the result of the document is what the reader would expect, then it may not be necessary to explain everything in detail. On the other hand, you could replace the term of art with a full definition of it or provide a definition outside the main text.

So, though some of the peculiarities of legal language are necessary and useful, this 'genuine' legal style is a tiny proportion of what makes the usual gobbledygook unclear. Within these limits, plain English law works as well as, if not better than, traditional legal language.

The proof of the pudding

When Assemblyman Peter Sullivan put forward New York's plain language law in 1980, its enemies were predicting chaos. Lawyers, banks and estate agents were all confidently expecting a deluge of lawsuits as soon as 'new' plain legal language replaced language that had been tested in the courts. Nothing happened. Very quickly, and with remarkable ease, companies rewrote their consumer contracts into intelligible English. They did it because they had to.

By 1984 the law had resulted in only two prosecutions by members of the public and one company – Lincoln Savings Bank – being forced by the Attorney General to rewrite a document. And the expected flood of lawsuits? It hasn't happened. If you need further proof that plain English works in the law, this is it.

As two American experts have put it: 'We now have over five years' experience since the first breakthrough consumer agreements in simple English were put into use. The authors are aware of no failure of enforceability resulting from the use of plain language.'[4]

Plain English Campaign has been writing legal documents in plain English for years. We have yet to encounter the mythical inadequacy of plain legal language. And the American example is now 18 years old.

We began this chapter by asking: 'Can the law survive without traditional legal language?' In an increasingly competitive legal market and with lawyers (particularly in America) concerned more than ever with improving their image, we should perhaps ask: 'How much longer can the law survive *with* traditional legal language?' We will be looking at these issues – money and the image of the law – in the next two chapters.

---

1 Richard Wydick, *Plain English for Lawyers*, pages 20-21.

2 Two of these examples are open to question. 'Give', 'devise' and 'bequeath' do each have slightly different technical meanings, though, in wills at least, 'give' will cover all three. Similarly, 'goods' and 'chattels' have technically different meanings. But 'chattels' includes 'goods', and the two are often used as if they mean the same thing.

3 Joseph Kimble, 'Plain English: A Charter for Clear Writing', *Thomas M Cooley Law Review* (9:1), page 20.

4 C. Felsenfield and A. Siegel – quoted in Richard Thomas, *Plain words for Consumers*, page 45.

Chapter 4

...one need not be a Marxist...

Making money out of plain English

> 'A compilation of words and turns of speech which has no other purpose than to be at hand at the right time where thought and positive knowledge are lacking.'
>
> Frederick Engels (joint author of *The Communist Manifesto*) defines 'jargon'.

Plain English law can do the job of legal gobbledygook and can help to do the job better. Legally, plain English stands up under cross-examination. But lawyers are always writing in a context. In particular, almost all legal writing is ruled over by one thing: money. If we are to make a case for plain English in the law, we must look at its balance sheet.

Does writing legal documents and letters in plain English cost more? And how do we measure the costs and rewards of plain English in the law? We will try to answer these questions in this chapter.

Counting the minutes

In any kind of business, time is money. And with lawyers charging their clients up to £100 an hour and more, every minute counts.

Surely it's quicker to write plain, simple everyday English?

As Richard Thomas, then legal officer at the National Consumer Council, points out, 'it comes more naturally' to write 'to repay my loan, I promise to pay you...' than 'for value received, the undersigned hereby promises to pay...'. If it comes more naturally, does it come more quickly? As Thomas points out:

> It would be foolish to pretend that writing in plain English is easy. It is usually more difficult to write simply and to the point than it is to waffle. Many lawyers will have difficulty, at first, in switching to a plain English style.

Professor Joseph Kimble, an American expert on legal clarity, agrees that 'just writing plainly is a worthy and difficult goal'. He warns:

> The greater part of clear writing only looks easy. It takes training and work and fair time to compose – all parts of the lawyer's craft.

If we could find a lawyer in, as it were, a virgin state, perhaps he or she would just sit down and write 'to repay my loan, I promise to pay you...'. But there are precious few such writers out there.

When lawyers working to a deadline turn to 'precedents' (standard legal agreements which can then be adapted), they find legalese. (There are very few books of precedents in plain English.) When lawyers read a statute or the account of a case, they find legalese. And all those years ago, when they really were virgin writers, law school and then employers quickly loaded them with enough jargon and bad writing style to overwhelm all but the most courageous.

That's the first point. Nothing really 'comes naturally' and plain English, while it may be what every lawyer tends to speak in normal life, is not the 'natural' language of the law. When there are more standard documents available in plain English, and plain English alternatives to standard legal wordings are more widely known, that will change. At the moment, any lawyer writing in plain English is swimming against the tide.

Second, the situation is rarely one in which you can compare writing in plain English and writing legalese. Often, the choice is between re-using the old rubbish or going back to square one to write in plain English. It should be obvious that, in this situation, plain English is going to take more thought, more time and so more money. And it should also be obvious that any company wanting to re-write its consumer contracts in plain English rather than do nothing, will have to pay to do so. Change will always cost money at first.

Third, is it more difficult to write simply and to the point than it is to waffle? Yes, because to write simply and to the point you must think through what you need to communicate with particular clarity and organise it in your head with particular care. Clear writing and clear thought go hand in hand. For most lawyers, writing simply and to the point is a habit that will take a while to pick up.

But remember what Wydick said about the time it takes to slay the monsters of legal jargon (chapter 3). It takes time, but those monsters stay dead. For the moment, plain English will take longer. Lawyers who are not already thinking carefully, clearly and with the reader in mind, will find that plain English forces them into doing so, and that will take time. But, as the tide turns, it *will* be quicker and cheaper, as the lay person might expect, to write plain English.

Counting the pennies

For the moment, writing plain English will take more time and so cost more. But we must set against this a whole heap of financial advantages in using plain English, some obvious, some subtle.

Plain English is quicker to read. This is so obvious that we need to say it again. The time saved when you can easily understand a piece of legal writing helps everyone. A clear letter from a solicitor will save their client valuable time.

Companies which re-write their contracts into plain English discover that their staff, as well as their customers, spend less time trying to understand the legal language and more time doing business.[1]

And how much would lawyers benefit if judges' opinions, laws, lawyers' presentations of cases and everything else were clear and to the point? The possible time savings, even rated at a mid-range fee of £100 an hour, suggest frighteningly large amounts of money are being poured down the drain every working day.

Plain English actually raises the quality of legal writing. As we discussed in chapter 3, legalese hides mistakes and unclear thinking.

Look at point three of the document at the start of chapter 1. The word 'equal' was taken out of paragraph 3 after 'Laura Smith' pointed out that later in the document the actual division of her 'interest in the Wood Mill' was not equal at all.

And part of the rest of that document reads:

> a) As to Miss Smith's share the total of all monies paid by her to SaveFast Home Loans Limited by way of mortgage repayment plus half the difference between the amount outstanding on the Mortgage and the said mortgage repayments and the sale price achieved.

This requires you to work out the difference between *three* things. (The 'difference' is what you have left when you take one number away from another. There is no such thing as the difference between three numbers.) Presumably, the writer meant to say:

. . . half the difference between:

> 1 the amount outstanding on the Mortgage plus the mortgage repayments; and

2 the sale price achieved.

Or

. . . half the difference between:

1 the amount outstanding on the Mortgage; and
2 the mortgage repayments plus the sale price achieved.

But the writer, drowning in legalese, didn't have time to make it clear which.

We don't think lawyers are generally incompetent – far from it. But everyone makes mistakes – everyone sometimes has to hurry through a job. Long muddled sentences and meaningless jargon make mistakes more likely and more difficult to spot.

Do you read and understand everything in every legal document you sign or, if you're a lawyer, every document you use?

Gobbledygook is fertile soil and a hiding ground for mistakes. And those mistakes cost money.

Readers and users of plain English documents are better informed.

Companies that re-write their forms find very quickly that they save money because they don't have to handle bewildered customers' questions any more.

> Southern California Gas Company simplified its billing statement and is saving an estimated $252,000 a year from reduced customer inquiries. [2]

Plain English produces consumer contracts that people actually read. They don't waste their time and the company's time by asking questions they don't need to ask, making complaints they don't need to make and, with insurance policies, making claims they have no hope of receiving. Because a document is in plain English, people actually have more respect for it. For an honest company, an informed customer is a trouble-free customer. When they rewrite their legal documents in plain English, companies are often shocked to find how little of the original their own staff understood. Plain English documents cut down on staff errors, time for administration and the need to train staff to understand baffling legalese. And companies using plain English have to call in expert advice less often.

Clearer documents make it:

- less likely that confusion will cause disputes;

- easier to settle disputes without going to court; and so

- less likely that disputes will go to court.

For lawyers writing to their clients, gobbledygook sometimes really costs.

> A firm of solicitors was . . . ordered to pay £95,000 damages for giving 'disastrous' advice to a client. A badly worded letter from the solicitors misled a property company client into thinking that a lease could not be terminated and that the existing tenants could stay on at the same rent until 1986. Part of the letter was phrased in 'very obscure' English, according to Mr Justice Jupp [the judge]; it was not surprising that the recipient, who was not a lawyer, misunderstood it.[3]

Lawyers who can communicate the law clearly are better able to fulfil their clients' wishes. If a client wants a particular agreement written, the lawyer writing in plain English can work with the client on equal ground. The task of negotiating the document is therefore quicker and cheaper.

The people who are paying lawyers to do a job (their bosses in a company, their clients, or the taxpayer in the case of the writers of laws) have a right to understand what they are paying for. Not least because, if they can't, it could well be wrong.

As what we've just said suggests, **plain English improves the relationship between the writer and the reader.** Legalese insults the reader. It says, 'Your time is less important than mine. I'm not going to try to make this understandable. You can spend time doing that.'

This attitude is illustrated perfectly in the following extracts from correspondence between a London-based small business and the local council's legal department. The owners of the business ran a shop, and rented the building from the council. The council sent them a 30-page lease, which was full of legalese and began with a sentence 126 words long. The owners could not understand what they were being asked to sign, and objected to having to pay for legal advice.

> Whilst we understand that the council's legal department may well speak a completely different language from the rest of the country, we fail to understand why we should have to stand the expense of getting it translated.

And here is part of the reply from the council's legal officer.

> Referring to the first and penultimate paragraphs of your letter, I can only state that if you feel that you are unable to comprehend the document in its current form, may I suggest or strongly advise that you contact your own independent legal adviser for explanation of the contents thereto.
>
> As regards to the document being transferred into 'Queen's English', without appearing to be difficult, I would inform you that I am at a loss as to what exactly your requirements are.

Or course, how stupid of the owners! All they needed to do was to pay their own solicitor to translate what the council's solicitor had written.

Writing in plain English, whether in a consumer contract or in a letter to a client, shows that you care about your reader. One Australian life insurance company comments:

> The plain English trust deed is user-friendly and can be understood. Our sales staff give it to potential customers early in the selling process, instead of after the sale has been made. This builds a sense of trust and openness. The new approach could not work with documents written in traditional legalese.[4]

Which brings us finally to this: **Plain English attracts customers.** Ever since Citibank in New York simplified its customer loan forms in the late 1970s, companies have found that plain English is a good selling point. Companies which write their consumer contracts in plain English tell everyone about it.

It's that bit easier to sell an insurance policy which both customer and salesperson can understand. And customers are very quickly put off by incomprehensible documents. In a world of ever more frantic competition, a sincere effort to communicate makes a real difference to that all-important factor: company image. For many companies, their commitment to plain English is a vital part of a wider commitment to fair dealing.

In the USA, many law firms across the country offer plain English legal writing services. Lawyers in the UK have been able to advertise their services for several years now. As a real market in legal services develops, lawyers will find that plain English is one service that makes them stand out from the crowd.

The Stark truth

The initial cost of working towards plain English pays off
remarkably quickly. Business after business is making the
change. But, before we finish discussing plain English and
money, we must look at two worries about plain English.

Firstly, the truth can sometimes hurt. Plain English, business
people fear, will reveal the unpleasant risks in a contract. A
contract written in legalese can seem to soften the impact of
a hard deal. But it can also hide more dubious parts of an
unfair one. There is no real justification for using legalese to
'protect' people from the unpleasant truth. If what is revealed
is unfair, then it should be seen to be so. And if the consumer
(or the business person) must confront some unpleasant
truths about standard business practice, then it is better that
they should adjust to the truth than that the lawyers should
hide the truth in legalese.

It is an inevitable consequence of our society's ever greater
emphasis on consumer choice that a consumer will have to
see more clearly, for example, the risks of a loan secured on
their home. We consumers have asked for clearer information
and, if we don't like some of it, we'll have to learn to live with
it, or go elsewhere.

And here is the second worry for lawyers.

> Lawyers write badly because doing so promotes their
> economic interests . . . One need not be a Marxist to
> understand that jargon helps professionals to convince
> the world of their occupational importance, which leads
> to payment for services.[5]

Steven Stark, in an article called 'Why lawyers can't write',
suggests that legalese actually helps lawyers collect their fees
because it convinces the rest of us that they are worth it.
He's criticising the lawyers, but lawyers are defending

themselves with exactly the same arguments. Reed Dickerson, an expert on legal writing in the USA, writes:

> Judge Harold Leventhal's observation that simplifying private instruments [legal documents] would make it harder to charge what they are worth is relevant but not persuasive. [6]

Dickerson rightly throws out Judge Leventhal's point because it 'too readily becomes an excuse for the status quo'. But we suspect a lot of lawyers would share Judge Leventhal's fear.

There is some truth in the Judge's point of view. Maybe some people will think a 'will' is worth less than a 'last will and testament'. But that is no excuse for legalese or higher fees.

In the first place, the lawyers have to ask themselves 'are we overcharging?' Second, and more importantly, they must learn not to retreat into legalese, but to communicate more clearly. If a lawyer explains *why* a document costs what it costs, then the client is unlikely to complain. People should be paying for a lawyer's knowledge of the law and ability to use it, not for his or her fluency in legalese.

Moreover, the situation may be changing. For a long time people have felt a mixture of irritation and respect in the face of unclear legal language. But, partly because of the plain English movement:

> Where once the mystery and incantations of legal concepts and language may have set the lawyer (and his business clients) apart by virtue of respect and/or fear, such feelings are more recently shifting to ridicule. [7]

Ridicule and anger: many people already agree with Steven Stark that legalese is a cynical money-spinner.

1 If you need proof, try, for example, the Law Reform Commission of Victoria's tests on the time it took lawyers and law students to understand plain English statutes: between a third and a half of the time they took to understand the old versions. See Law Reform Commission of Victoria, Australia *Plain English and the Law*, pages 67-70.

2 Joseph Kimble, 'Plain English: A Charter for Clear Writing', *Thomas M Cooley Law Review,* (9:1), page 26.

3 Richard Thomas and Liz Dunbar, *Plain English for lawyers*, page 4.

4 John Warburton, OAMPS Ltd, client of Phillips Fox Solicitors, Melbourne, Australia.

5 Steven Stark, Harvard Law Professor. *Harvard Law Review*, Vol 97, pages 1389-93.

6 Reed Dickerson, *The Fundamentals of Legal Drafting*, page 166.

7 Martin Fingerhut, 'The Plain English Movement in Canada,' *Canadian Business Law Journal* 6 1981-2, page 448.

Chapter 5

...the truth, the whole truth, and nothing but the truth...

Beauty, image and the language of the law

We have discussed why legal language has ended up in its present state. And we have argued that lawyers must use plain English because:

- it works better;

- it is required by law in consumer contracts;

- it is right to do so;

- it is good for business; and

- it saves money.

Two related points remain. One is the lawyers' last defence of traditional legal language: that plain English will destroy the beauty of legal language. The other concerns the effect of legal language, plain or mystifying, on the image of the law.

Majesty of the law

The lay person: Beauty of legal language? You're kidding. You'll be telling me bus timetables are great literature next.

The lawyer: Yes, beauty. Language isn't *just* about communication. Language can create an atmosphere, it can make you angry, it can make you cry. Sometimes the language of the law needs to do one of those things: in a speech to a court, to make you feel anger at a crime.

Or in the oath that every witness
has to swear, to make them feel the
seriousness of what they are doing.

The lay person:	Carry on.

The lawyer:	OK. The oath. Everyone who gives evidence in court has to swear that they'll tell the truth, the whole truth, and nothing but the truth. This all started because the medieval Christian philosopher, Saint Thomas Aquinas, said that an oath to tell the truth wasn't an oath to tell the whole truth.

The lay person:	Not a very saintly thing to say.

The lawyer:	We all have our off days. Anyway, it's pretty obvious that Thomas's point isn't really relevant today. And most people would accept that an oath to tell the truth doesn't mean 'tell the truth and some lies as well'.

The lay person:	So we don't really need to say 'the whole truth and nothing but the truth'. It's just more waffle.

The lawyer:	Precisely. You see, I've heard the rest of this and I know that there's a whole load of worthless repetition in legalese. And yet 'the truth, the whole truth, and nothing but the truth' still has a value. When witnesses say those words, they feel the seriousness of what they are about to do. 'The truth, the whole truth and nothing but the truth' is a vital part of the majesty of the law. And

these plain English people want each witness to say 'I promise to tell the truth'.

Plain English Campaign: (PEC)	Not so fast. Plain English isn't about stamping on good writing and powerful language. We have nothing against 'the truth, the whole truth, and nothing but the truth'. Most witnesses who take that oath know exactly what it means. And the few who don't should have it explained to them.
The lawyer:	So you're not against throwing words around a bit?
PEC:	We're not *against* using words powerfully, no. We're *for* clear English. There's a place in plain English law for 'the truth, the whole truth, and nothing but the truth'. And there's a place for making people angry or making them cry, if that's what you need to do. Plain English has always recognised that there's more to language than communication. And we're not just talking about courtroom speeches. If you're a solicitor writing a letter to someone about a divorce, it's no good just stating your case. The way you write will have a powerful effect on how your reader feels.
The lawyer:	But isn't plain English a bit flat?
PEC:	We don't think so. Remember what we said in the introduction: 'plain' doesn't mean ugly, dull or unsophisticated. Plain English has a beauty of its own. Plain English has a long literary history which includes Francis Bacon, Mark Twain, George Orwell, Winston Churchill and our old friend Jonathan Swift. None of

these writers thought that plain English was second best.

The lay person: This doesn't seem to be about law at all. How can you talk about literature when I'm faced with this contract for my dishwasher which I can't understand?

PEC: We were just trying to make the point that plain English can be a powerful writing style. You're half right about your dishwasher contract. Yes, there's less room for 'literary effect' in a consumer contract. But whether you're buying a dishwasher by hire purchase or telling a jury that Joe Bloggs is innocent, clarity has a force all of its own. Look at our example from chapter 3. Which of these impresses you more?

> The due observance and fulfilment of the terms so far as they relate to anything to be done or complied with by the Insured and the truth of the statements and answers in the Proposal shall be conditions precedent to any liability of the Company to make any payment under this policy.

Or:

> We will only make a payment under this Policy if:
>
> • you have kept to the terms of the Policy; and

- the statements and answers in your Proposal are true.

Which one is a bit flat? Which one is more commanding? And how would each of them make you feel about your insurance company?

The lay person:	I take your point.
PEC:	There is room for extra flourishes like 'the whole truth' and so on, within limits. But plain English isn't 'Peter and Jane' baby talk. It doesn't just do the job better than legalese, it actually sounds better: more clear-headed, more business-like. Clarity is a great persuader.
	Besides, the *first* job of legal language is to communicate clearly and precisely. It's no good writing a beautiful speech defending a criminal if half the jury don't understand it. No one is going to write to you from jail praising your fancy writing style. Which takes us back to chapter 3. Plain English simply does the job better.
The lawyer:	Let me get this straight. Plain English can do the job of traditional legal language. And the improved clarity actually helps to avoid mistakes. Since 1 July 1995, consumer contracts in the UK have had to be in clear and intelligible language. Unclear legal language is immoral. It wastes millions of pounds a year. And plain English has a powerful literary past going back to the Renaissance.
PEC:	That's a fair summary.

The lawyer:	And I suppose you're going to tell me that unclear legal language is to blame for the way people feel about lawyers?
PEC:	I'm afraid so. You know as well as I do that lawyers in America now have a very serious image problem. And it has spread across the Atlantic. Legalese is a crucial part of that bad image.
The lawyer:	But my clients and colleagues expect me to use traditional legal language.
PEC:	Some of them, perhaps. As we said in chapter 1, legalese is part of today's image of the lawyer. But remember two things. One, that it's up to you to make the change and justify it to your clients. You'll need to convince (and convert) your colleagues too. Two, don't assume you can't survive without gobbledygook. You may well find that your clients and your colleagues are pleased to get a document they can understand easily. Attitudes are changing. One survey in California found that judges, presented with briefs written in legalese and in plain English, thought that the lawyers writing the legalese 'possessed less professional prestige than those who wrote in plain English'[1] The problem with the image of the law isn't that people are crying out for legalese. Too many of them know there's an alternative. Listen to this top American lawyer, Bryan Garner. 'There's probably no single reform that would improve the image of lawyers more than to get them to speak plainly and directly and understandably.'[2]

Many lay people have already come to the

same opinion as Steven Stark. (See chapter 4.) They think that lawyers write badly because they get paid more for seeming clever and because they and other lawyers get paid for deciphering the bad writing.

The lay person: It had crossed my mind.

The lawyer: Oh. Well . . . I guess that settles it. But where do I go from here?

PEC: The guide to writing plain legal English in chapter 6. That might be a good place to start.

---

1 Joseph Kimble, 'Plain English: A Charter for Clear Writing', *Thomas M Cooley Law Review*, (9:1), page 24

2 Kimble, page 27

Chapter 6

Writing plain legal English

Introduction

The earlier chapters have put forward the arguments for using a plain English style. The rest of this book tells you how to go about doing it.

We do not pretend it is easy, but it is possible.

Clear legal writing depends on:

- a clear understanding of the law;

- a clear interpretation of the law; and

- a clear expression of the law.

You should not need any help from us with the first two items on this list. We will give you a set of guidelines to help you express your ideas clearly and accurately. These guidelines are tried and tested, and have helped thousands of writers (and readers) in all walks of life. We will ask you to examine your writing style in some detail.

But we will not ask you to ignore your legal training. The better you understand the law and the issues involved, the easier you will find it to write plain legal English.

At the end of each section you will find a number of exercises. When you have finished each set, compare your answers with our suggested answers at the end of the book.

Section 1

Think of your reader and use an appropriate writing style

It may seem obvious to suggest that you start by thinking of your reader and trying to gauge your reader's level of understanding. Yet how little we see this happen in practice!

There will be times when you are writing for your peers and colleagues, and you will know exactly what you have to explain and what you don't. But if you are writing to a lay person, you need to give much more thought to their level of knowledge, education and literacy.

- Picture your reader. Where do they live? What do they do for a living? Are they young or old? How articulate are they?

- What do they already know about the subject?

Wearing your legal hat, decide what it is that you have to say and then say it clearly.

Your letter to a client is a a good place to start because, having met them, you are much more likely to be able to gauge their level of understanding. Also, the letter is a one-off piece of writing and is not affected by form or precedent.

Here are our guidelines, to help you form an appropriate style.

Write as you would talk to your reader

Always try to imagine that you are *talking* to your reader, and your tone and language will become more appropriate.

Writers lose many of their bad habits when they speak. We will look at these bad habits later and give you positive guidelines for avoiding them.

Use everyday language wherever you can

Legal writing should use everyday English unless there is a good reason to use less familiar words.

There are many words that have legal flavouring but add nothing to the legality (or the clarity) of a piece of writing: 'said', 'aforesaid', 'herein', 'aforementioned', 'hereinafter', 'forthwith', 'hereinbefore', 'heretofore' to name but a few. Many lawyers use these words believing that they are more precise than commoner words. But, as we discussed in chapter 3, words like 'said' and 'aforementioned' offer only phoney precision and a legalistic flavour. Cut them out.

If a client comes to see you about a divorce, they might not know what you are talking about if you write to them confirming their 'instructions'. They might be surprised to see that the letter is headed:

Re: Matrimonial

or even worse:

Re: Your matrimonial affairs

especially if they view themselves as the injured party!

Always ask yourself 'Does my letter really need a heading?' After all, your client will already know why they went to see you.

Use personal words like 'I', 'we' and 'you'.

These 'personal reference words' relax the writing and help the reader to feel involved and considered. Official writing of all kinds often ignores these words. As a result, the reader is referred to as 'the applicant', 'the tenant', 'the claimant', 'the insured'. The writer becomes 'the council', 'the bank', 'the authority' and so on.

When you are writing a formal letter you can still say:

> Thank you for your letter. . .
> I was sorry to hear. . .
> We are able to lend you. . .
> Please let me know if I can. . .

Remember that there is a real person at the receiving end of your letter and that they may be upset, worried or frightened.

Let's put these ideas together. Imagine that your client has signed an authority for you to get some information from a solicitor who acted for them in the past. Would you write your letter like this?

Re: Matrimonial

With reference to the return of the authority duly signed, I have written to your former Solicitors requesting your will and title deeds to Fleet Mill. As it was stated in the interview that the aforesaid property was in mortgage, the said title deeds should properly be held by the mortgagees.

Perhaps you would. After all, this is a normal solicitor's letter, isn't it? But if you think about the *reader*, you will realise the following:

- There's no need for the heading. A letter like this should be self-explanatory.

- The letter does not even say 'thank you' for signing and returning the form - a basic courtesy.

- The tone is heavy because of the 'formal' words it uses – 'duly', 'interview', 'said', 'aforesaid', 'in mortgage', and 'mortgagees'.

You may ask 'What is wrong with the word 'interview'? Surely that's plain enough?' Yes it is. But you are forgetting the reader. You will have viewed the encounter as an 'interview', but to the reader it may simply have been a case of getting a load of troubles off their chest. Put yourself in their shoes and see the message from *their* point of view.

See what you think of our suggestion.

Dear Mrs Power

Thank you for signing the authority for me to contact Smith and Jones for the documents we need. I have now asked them to send me your will and the title deeds to your cottage, Fleet Mill.

However, as you told me that you have a mortgage, we should probably pass the title deeds to XYZ Building Society when we receive them.

This letter is professional and includes all the relevant information, but is more relaxed and clearer than the original.

Forms can be human too

When you design forms or questionnaires, don't artificially shorten instructions by leaving out key words like 'a' and 'the'. If you want a sensible answer, ask a sensible question. We see the following 'questions' on forms all too often:

> Name of Claimant.
> DOB
> Na Ins No.
> Ret'd.
> State pension.

Don't expect the first-time user of a form to be able to decipher this type of code and give the information you need. For example in the last item, do you want them to state the amount of their pension, or to give the amount of their state pension? The two may often be different. Or do you want them to indicate whether they receive a state pension? The chances are that you won't get the information you want.

Remember to write to your reader as you would talk. If your reader was sitting opposite you, would you ask, 'What is your DOB?' If common sense suggests that a question would sound patronising ('What is your name?' for instance), make sure the reader knows exactly what information you want.

So our list of questions would become:

> Your name.
> Your date of birth.
> Your National Insurance number.
> Are you retired?
> Please say how much pension you get each month.

Don't forget – a happy client is good for business.

Summary

- **Write as you would talk to your reader.**

- **Use everyday language wherever you can.**

- **Use personal words like 'I', 'we', and 'you'.**

- **Don't artificially shorten words and phrases.**

Exercises

Re-write the following examples in more everyday language, using the guidelines we have covered in this section.

1 From a solicitor's letter to a client

In consequence of your verbal instructions via the telephone I have to advise you that I have written to Messrs Small and Co to inform them of your intention to terminate the contract.

Although I do not expect this to necessitate further correspondence, it will be appreciated that this is subject to a favourable response from the aforementioned company.

2 From a solicitor's letter to a graphic designer

If you could let me have the latest typed version of the form in the next seven days, whereupon I suggest we meet again to discuss. Work on the design could proceed in parallel to this and I would be grateful for a mock-up at your earliest convenience.

3 From a transport company letter to a member of the public

With reference to your recent letter about the provision of a public bus shelter in Devon Lane. You may be aware that shelter erection at all sites has been constrained in recent years as a result of our budgetary allocation from district councils. Although it seems that the budget for shelter provision will be enhanced in the forthcoming financial year, it is axiomatic that those prospective sites that have been on the waiting list for long periods will be considered more favourably.

Section 2

Write 'actively'

The simplest and clearest sentences tend to have just three parts:

- Agent
- Verb
- Object

Forgive us if you already know all this. But it is suprising how many people don't.

Verbs are normally described as 'doing' words, because we use them to describe actions. So in the following sentences, the words in bold type are verbs:

The clerk **typed** the letter.

The dog **bit** the doctor.

The camel **drank** the water.

The **agent** is the 'doer'. In other words, they are the person or thing performing the action. So in the following sentences, the words in bold type are the agents:

The **clerk** typed the letter.

The **dog** bit the doctor.

The **camel** drank the water.

Lastly, the **object** is the person or thing the action is being done to. So in the following sentences, the words in bold type are the objects:

The clerk typed the **letter**.

The dog bit the **doctor.**

The camel drank the **water**.

The 'agent – verb – object' arrangement is significant, because this is the order in which we are most used to getting information. It is the word order we tend to use when we speak. In this kind of sentence the verb is said to be **active,** or in the 'active voice'.

Suppose we tinker with the word order in our examples:

The letter was typed by the clerk.

The doctor was bitten by the dog.

The water was drunk by the camel.

Now the agents come after the verbs, and the verbs themselves have become more complex - 'was typed', 'was bitten' and 'was drunk'.

By changing the word order we have changed the nature of the verbs. Now the verb is said to be **passive,** or in the 'passive voice.'

Prefer the active to the passive

Usually you can express ideas much more clearly and concisely with an active voice. The reader can see straight away who, or what, is performing the action in the sentence, because the agent is the first thing they read.

So prefer the active to the passive unless you have a good reason to use the passive. Active verbs tend to keep sentences short and make writing more lively and direct. Using too many passive verbs tends to make writing cold, impersonal and bureaucratic.

We're not saying 'never use passive verbs'. Passive verbs can be more appropriate in some situations where they soften a blunt message or spread responsibility.

Here are two of the most common uses of passives.

When an active might sound hostile

'You have not paid the premium' may sound too hostile or aggressive to the reader. You may want to soften this by using passive verbs: 'Your premium has not been paid.'

When you want to spread responsibility or avoid blaming someone

'A mistake was made in working out your bill' avoids admitting that 'I made a mistake. . .' or 'We made a mistake. . .' and so on.

But be careful when you do use the passive, because it can leave the meaning unclear, as in the following sentence.

> It is feared that adequate steps will not be taken to mitigate the shareholders' losses.

This leaves the reader asking a number of questions:

> Who fears that adequate steps will not be taken? The shareholders? The writer? Or perhaps someone else?

> Who ought to be taking the steps? The shareholders? Someone else?

The problem is that passive verbs do not need agents. Writers often leave out the agents for passive verbs. This forces readers to supply their own – and they often guess incorrectly.

Try to keep the agent – verb – object order

Try not to interrupt the agent – verb – object arrangement because the reader will search for this, and will understand more quickly if the three are kept close together.

It is easy to keep to this word order in a simple construction. But as sentences get more dense, with overlapping ideas which modify, qualify or explain, the basic elements can get pushed further and further apart.

For instance:

> The solicitor, who had been waiting for the client to supply all the information that she could get hold of about her husband's income and outgoings, prepared the affidavit.

A chunk of 25 words disturbs the structure of the sentence as follows by sitting between the agent and the verb.

You can deal with this in two different ways. In a sentence like this one, which contains only one major idea, restructure the sentence to bring the agent – verb – object together:

> After the client had given all the information she could about her husband's income and outgoings, the solicitor prepared the affidavit.

In some cases however the sentence just contains too much information.

For instance:

> The accused, who has been charged with fatally shooting his girlfriend when she was sitting in the back of her employer's new company car, wishes to present to the court evidence that he had an unhappy childhood.

In these cases, split the information up into two sentences, keeping the agent – verb – object together in both.

The court has charged the accused with fatally shooting his girlfriend when she was sitting in the back of her employer's new company car. The accused wishes to present evidence to the court that he had an unhappy childhood.

We'll discuss sentence length more fully in section 4.

When describing an action, use a verb

'What else would I use?' you may ask. Having said earlier that verbs are 'doing' words, that's a reasonable question. But consider the following sentences.

The decision has been taken by the Board.

The implementation of the report will be undertaken by a small team.

We had a discussion about legal writing.

What are the verbs in these sentences? Do they describe what is happening in each case?

The verbs are: 'has been taken'; 'will be undertaken'; and 'had'.

Although they are 'doing' words they do not describe what is actually happening.

Here are the same ideas, but expressed differently.

The Board has decided.

A small team will implement the report.

We discussed legal writing.

Now it is easier to see what has happened. This wasn't so clear because in the original versions the verb 'decided' had become 'the decision', the verb 'implement' had become 'the implementation of', and the verb 'discussed' had become 'a discussion'.

These expressions are known as 'nominalisations' or 'nouns formed from verbs'. Because we need a verb to make the sentences work, we have to invent one. But, as you can see from the examples above, the verbs don't actually say what is happening.

Nominalisations have the effect of beating about the bush, as if the actual verb is considered to be too straightforward or blunt. Sometimes lawyers (and other writers) use nominalisations to hide an unpleasant fact or to blur the edges of a raw verb.

So:

Lawyers don't act – they take action.
They don't argue – they present an argument.
They don't assume – they make assumptions.
They don't conclude – they draw conclusions.
They make statements and raise objections.

And so on. . .

The two sentences below say the same thing, but the second uses verbs to describe the action while the first uses nominalisations.

> The decision which has been reached by my client is that if there is a continuation of your action in this manner, the termination of the contract will be taken into serious consideration by her. (35 words)

> My client has decided that if you continue to act in this way, she will seriously consider ending the contract. (20 words)

Notice how we can say 'ending' rather than 'the termination of'. Nominalisations are often inflated versions of the verbs they are derived from. For instance, 'to use' becomes 'the utilisation of'.

Use nominalisations sparingly as too many produce stodgy, dull and unclear writing.

Nominalisations also tend to appear with passive verbs which is another reason for avoiding them.

Summary

- **Prefer the active voice to the passive voice.**

- **Try to keep the agent – verb – object together and in order.**

- **When describing an action, use a verb.**

Exercises

Using the guidelines we have covered in this section, re-write the following examples. Remember the 'agent – verb – object' word order. You will need to use it when changing passive verbs into active ones.

1 From a letter to a client.

The form was sent to you at the address that was supplied to us. However, it was returned by the Post Office as 'undeliverable mail'.

(Hint: you will need to invent agents for the two verbs in the first sentence. So assume that your company has sent the form to the client, and that the client has supplied the address.)

2   From a Surveyor's letter

The problem can be solved by the removal of the plaster to a
height of one metre, the insertion of a new damp proof
course, and the introduction of suitable floor joists.

3   From a letter giving notice to an employee

You are under an obligation to work during this period of
notice. Failure to do so will result in the stoppage of pay for
each day not worked.

4   From a council report

Further to the above we recommend that, subject to there
being sufficient funds in the budget, and the necessary
agreement being obtained from Personnel Department,
employees be canvassed to seek their interest in accepting
voluntary early retirement.

(Hint: you may find it helps to split this into two sentences.)

Section 3

Be positive

This doesn't mean saying 'yes' when you mean 'no'. But often we find that ideas are expressed in a negative way for no good reason.

For instance:

> If you do not sign the document, we will not be able to exchange contracts.

This may be appropriate if earlier letters have been ignored. But as a first approach, why not write:

> Please sign the document so that we can exchange contracts.

This sounds much more positive.

Lawyers are trained to look for difficulties and problems, so this may be the reason for a rather gloomy writing style. If you find yourself writing a negative sentence when there is some good news in there somewhere, try taking out the negatives and making your ideas positive. It might brighten up your day – as well as the reader's.

Exercises

Bring out the positive aspects of these messages.

1 Failure to give a wide choice of dates may result in a delayed hearing.

2 No one may take part in the arbitration hearing unless they are one of the affected parties or their legal representative.

3 We value each property not less often than once a year.

Section 4

Serve up your message in manageable chunks

In other words: Keep your sentences as short as you can.

Everybody can tell a horror story about a legal sentence with hundreds of words in it – and no punctuation. If a sentence is written that way, then changing it is like trying to defuse an unexploded bomb.

When writing from scratch, however, there are no excuses. Long sentences are the result of insufficient planning, poor writing technique and a total lack of thought for the reader.

Think of a sentence as a complete statement that could stand by itself. A sentence should generally contain one main point with perhaps one related point. If you are putting more than one idea in a sentence, think about ways of dividing the information into two or more sentences. Long sentences tend to contain too many separate ideas. This makes it difficult for the reader to pick out the main idea and to see what relationship other ideas have to it and to each other.

Look at the following little gem from the Benefits Agency.

> You get free National Health Service (NHS) dental treatment automatically while you are pregnant, provided you were pregnant at the start of the treatment, and for a year after your baby's birth.

There are 32 words in this sentence, so it is hardly enormous. There is nothing grammatically wrong either, and it is correctly punctuated.

But the writer has tried to cover the *duration* of the free treatment, and the *conditions* for getting it, in the same sentence. The verb 'get' is the second word in the sentence, yet the reader should also apply it to the last idea in the sentence: 'and for a year after your baby's birth.' Not surprisingly, the results are comical. (Anyone qualifying under this paragraph should also contact *The Guinness Book of Records*.)

Aim for an average sentence length of 15-20 words

Most experts agree that clear writing should have an average sentence length of 15-20 words. We often hear people say that this length is more difficult to keep to in legal writing because the sentence has to carry complicated information.

Yet many writers have to convey complicated ideas. All the following types of document have been written in plain English, and have kept to the 15-20 word average.

- Credit card terms and conditions.

- Business account terms and conditions.

- Life assurance policies proposal forms.

- Office equipment hire agreements.

- Leaflets aimed at the public about court procedures.

- Leaflets on divorce and separation.

Of course, in some of these areas plain English documents are still the exception rather than the rule. But the good examples show that it can be done. It is too easy to say that complicated ideas need complicated words and sentence structures to explain them.

Try to vary your writing by mixing short sentences with longer ones and following the basic principle of having one main idea in a sentence, plus perhaps one other related point.

The previous sentence has 31 words in it, and could be broken into two sentences. But it is not a difficult sentence to follow and shortening it would not make a lot of difference to its clarity. As with our other guidelines, don't follow the rule slavishly.

Or you can use lists

Using a list is one of the best ways of breaking down complex information into manageable chunks. Lists usually have two main parts:

- an introductory statement, sometimes called a signpost, because it indicates that a list is coming up; and
- the separate points or conditions.

If the points can stand alone and are complete sentences, start each one with a capital letter and end with a full stop. For example:

> For the rule to apply, all the following conditions must be met:

- The owner of the land must live abroad.
- The tenant occupying the land must pay rent to an agent registered in the UK.
- The land must be at least 10 hectares in area.

When you turn solid text into a list, all the things listed should normally begin with the same kind of word or phrase, otherwise the consistent structure of the list may break down. In the above list each item begins with an agent followed by a verb. You can use devices such as squares, bullet points or dashes to pick out the listed things.

Lists can be particularly helpful in legal writing because they help to break down conditional sentences. (Sentences like 'If X then Y.' Or 'When B happens, do C.')

These sentences can become complicated if they have several conditions, like the following:

Under the Law of Property Act 1925, a lease may be enlarged into a fee simple if there is not less than two hundred years of the lease unexpired; the lease was originally granted for at least three hundred years; no trust or right of redemption exists in favour of the reversioner; and no rent of any money value is payable.

We can make this into a list quite easily, because the first 17 words govern everything that follows.

Under the Law of Property Act 1925, a lease may be enlarged into a fee simple if:

● there is not less than two hundred years of the lease unexpired;

● the lease was originally granted for at least three hundred years;

● no trust or right of redemption exists in favour of the reversioner; and

● no rent of any money value is payable.

(We could, of course, also make this a lot clearer.)

With a bit of practice, you will soon get used to the technique and will find it a considerable help in arranging your ideas.

Summary

- **Keep your sentences as short as you can.**

- **Aim for an average sentence length of 15-20 words.**

- **Use lists to break down complex, conditional sentences.**

Exercises

Split these long sentences into shorter ones at appropriate points. You will need to add or remove words to mend the breaks you create. Use lists where you feel this will help.

1   From an internal report

Our present system of calculating overtime pay is manual and very time-consuming, and leads to extra costs because the wages staff have to check each calculation.

2   From a warning letter to an employee

I raised your difficulty about arriving ready for work on time and pointed out that your managers had done their best to take account of your travel problems and you had agreed with them that the Green Lane depot was the most convenient place for you to work, however, your initial improvement was short-lived and over the past two months your punctuality has dropped to a totally unacceptable level.

Section 5

Be concise

So many writers use five words when one will do. If your ideas are valid, there is no reason to dress them up.

If you begin paragraphs with 'Further to the above, I would advise that...', try getting on with the message without first clearing your throat.

Instead of writing	Why not write
with respect to	about
for the purpose of	to
prior to	before
at this point in time	now
subsequent to	after
in accordance with	under
by reason of	because

These phrases and others like them are common in legal writing. They slow up the writing and irritate the reader.

Beware of padding your writing with empty words and phrases, such as:

Clearly... (If it's clear, your readers will see for themselves.)

It is interesting to note that... (It either is or it isn't.)

It may be appropriate to point out that... (If it is, just point it out.)

As far as concerns this writer... (Get on with it!)

If you are expressing an opinion, rather than stating a fact, 'it is the opinion of this writer' is no more effective than 'I think' or 'I believe'.

As we discussed in Chapter 3, in most cases, these common legal phrases are unnecessary and confusing. Most of the legal 'doubles' and 'triples' can be replaced with one word.

- Will and testament

- Fit and proper

- Give, devise and bequeath

- Goods and chattels

- Any and all

- Save and expect

- Null and void

- Suffer or permit

- Rest, residue and remainder

- Force and effect

- Each and every

Exercises

Cut out useless words and shorten wordy phrases.

1   From an electricity company letter

The standing charge is payable in respect of each and every quarter.

2   From a surveyor's letter to a solicitor

Further to the above I would advise that I have written to the building society to advise them that the building has suffered structural damage.

3   From an engineering company's notice board

Upon the activation of the fire alarm evacuation of the premises by all personnel should take place immediately followed by assembly in the car park.

4   A sign in the car park of a public building

Persons leaving vehicles in this car park without the express permission of the proprietors shall be liable to have a clamp affixed thereto for the purpose of immobilising the same.

Section 6

Destroying some myths

We're not in favour of breaking grammatical **rules.** But we are irritated by writers who slavishly follow grammatical myths.

So let's knock down three of the most common ones.

- You **can** start a sentence with 'and', 'but', 'or', 'so', 'because', or 'however'.
- You **can** split infinitives. So you can say **to boldly go**.
- You **can** end a sentence with a preposition. In fact, it is something **we should stand up for**.

Starting sentences with words like 'and' and 'but'

Words like 'and', 'but', 'because', 'so', and 'or' are conjunctions. They link the clauses in a sentence.

> The solicitor was in court, *but* his client didn't turn up.

Many people believe that because conjunctions are 'joining words', they should not be used to start sentences. However, most good writers ignore the 'rule', believing that if conjunctions are meant to create links, they should be allowed to do so between one sentence and another as well as within sentences.

Ernest Gowers, in *The Complete Plain Words*, says:

> There used to be an idea that it was inelegant to begin a sentence with 'and'. The idea is now dead. And to use 'and' in this position may be a useful way of indicating that what you are about to say will reinforce what you have just said. 'But'... may be freely used to begin either a sentence or a paragraph.

You can split infinitives

The present tense of the infinitive is formed by 'to' plus the verb: 'to charge', 'to sentence', 'to appeal'. Any word put between the 'to' and the verb is said to split the infinitive, as in 'to boldly go.'

The 'rule' against splitting infinitives seems to have started with 19th century grammarians who wanted English to imitate Latin. In Latin, present tense infinitives are one word, not two, so it is impossible to split them.

Although some people may prefer the 'pure' form of keeping the infinitive intact, the split infinitive may make your sentence sound more rhythmical. What about:

> The appeal court was urged to more than double the sentence.

Can you rewrite this without splitting the infinitive and still avoid a clumsy construction?

You can end a sentence with a preposition

John Dryden seems to have decided that sentences should not end with prepositions. Again this was because of the comparison with Latin. As with split infinitives, grammarians of the time took up the idea and it has survived. The most common prepositions are: 'in', 'on', 'up', 'to', 'before', 'after', 'over', 'with', 'by', 'of' and 'from'. Technically, these words are not always prepositions. It depends on their role in the sentence.

The best guide is: 'Let a preposition stay at the end of the sentence if the sentence sounds more natural and rhythmical that way.'

Section 7

Conclusion

We hope you have found this book thought-provoking and useful. It won't change the way you write – only you can do that. But it should have given you a set of fairly simple techniques that you can apply to your writing.

Summary:

- Write as you would talk to your reader.
- Use personal words like 'I', 'we' and 'you'.
- Don't artificially shorten words and phrases.
- Prefer actives to passives.
- Try to keep the agent – verb – object together and in order.
- When describing an action, use a verb.
- Be positive.
- Write sentences averaging 15-20 words.
- Be concise. Cut out unnecessary words and phrases.
- Don't be a slave to out-dated grammatical myths.

Techniques are all very well, but first you may need to rethink your attitude to writing and to your readers. Your aim should always be to give a clear message. There is the temptation to score points, to impress, or simply to justify one's fee! But think of your reader – often they will be the person paying you to write in the first place.

Finally

We recently spoke to a manager in the head office of a mortgage brokers. He had just bought his first house, and during this stressful time had received a letter from his solicitor. Although no stranger to the house-buying business, the manager could not understand what the letter was telling him. So he phoned up to ask for an explanation. The reply was: "Of course we'll be happy to explain what the letter means, but there will be a charge of £50."

We leave you to decide whether this is an acceptable way of doing business.

Our suggested answers

In a few cases, our answers are the only ones possible. However, many can be written in several different ways. Also, bad writing can be ambiguous, so we may have interpreted the examples one way, you another.

Think about any differences between your answers and ours. Often the differences will be due to personal style, and there's nothing wrong with this. The last thing we want to do is produce writing 'clones' who all write in exactly the same way. But if our answer is:

- shorter;

- clearer;

- friendlier; or

- quicker at getting to the point,

then try to let more of our style rub off onto your writing.

Section 1

1   Following our telephone conversation I have written to Small and Co to tell them that you plan to end the contract.

I do not expect to have to write again, but this depends on their agreeing to our suggestions.

2   Please let me have the latest typed version of the form in the next seven days. We can then meet again. In the meantime, please start work on the design and let me have a mock-up as soon as you can.

(Although 'mock-up' is not an everyday word, a graphic designer would know what you mean.)

3   Thank you for your letter asking for a bus shelter in Devon Lane. As you may know, we have not been able to build many shelters in recent years because we have had less money from the district councils. We expect to get more money for shelters in the next financial year, starting in April.

However, we have a waiting list of sites. The longer a site has been on the waiting list, the more likely we are to build a shelter there.

Section 2

1   We sent the form to you at the address you gave us.
     However, the Post Office returned it as 'undeliverable
     mail'.

2   We can solve the problem by removing the plaster to a
     height of one metre, inserting a new damp proof course,
     and introducing suitable floor joists.

     Or

     We can solve the problem by removing the plaster to a
     height of one metre, and by putting in a new damp
     proof course and suitable floor joists.

3   You must work during this period of notice. You will not
     be paid for any day you do not work.

     Or (more bluntly)

     You must work during this period of notice. We will not
     pay you for any days you do not work.

4   We recommend that we canvass employees to find out
     if they are interested in accepting voluntary early
     retirement. We will first need to make sure there is
     enough money in the budget and that the Personnel
     Department agrees.

Section 3

1   Please give a wide choice of dates to get an early hearing.

    Or

The wider your choice of dates, the better your chance of an early hearing.

    Or

You will get an earlier hearing if you give a wide choice of dates.

2   You can only take part in the arbitration hearing if you are one of the affected parties or their legal representative.

3   We value each property at least once a year.

Section 4

1   Our present system of calculating overtime pay is manual and very time-consuming. It leads to extra costs because the wages staff have to check each calculation.

2   I raised your difficulty about arriving ready for work on time. I pointed out that your managers had done their best to take account of your travel problems and you had agreed with them that the Green Lane depot was the most convenient place for you to work. However, your initial improvement was short-lived. Over the past two months your punctuality has dropped to a totally unacceptable level.

Or

I raised your difficulty about arriving ready for work on time. I pointed out that:

●   your managers had done their best to take account of your travel problems; and

●   you had agreed with them that the Green Lane depot was the most convenient place for you to work.

However, your initial improvement was short-lived. Over the past two months your punctuality has dropped to a totally unacceptable level.

(If your version has a full stop after 'travel problems', think about how many things the writer is 'pointing out'.)

Section 5

1   The standing charge is payable each quarter.

or

The standing charge is payable quarterly.

or

The standing charge is payable for each quarter.

(You could use the active verb 'must pay', but this might sound too aggressive.)

2   I have written to the building society to tell them that the building has suffered structural damage.

3   If you hear the fire alarm, leave the building immediately and go to the car park.

or

If the fire alarm sounds, everyone must leave the building immediately and assemble in the car park.

4   If you leave your vehicle in this car park without our permission, it will be clamped.

(Again, you could use the active verb 'we will clamp it'. But often car park owners use a contractor to do the work.)

Further reading

Below are the full details of the books and articles which have helped us with this book. The ones marked with stars are particularly useful if you want to know more about plain English and the Law.

ALBSU, *Making it happen: Improving Basic Skills for the 21st Century*, 1994

Charlotte Low Allen, 'Skilled Legal Writing Becomes Exceptional', *Insight on the News*, Dec 25 1989 - Jan 1990

Francis Bennion, *Statute Law*, Longman, 1983 (2nd Edition)

Sir Rupert Cross, *Statutory Interpretation*, Butterworth, 1987 (2nd Edition by John Bell and Sir George Engle)

Reed Dickerson, *The Fundamentals of Legal Drafting*, Little, Brown and Company, 1986 (2nd Edition)

Martin Fingerhut, 'The Plain English Movement in Canada', *Canadian Business Law Journal*, Vol 6, 1981-2

Lord Simon of Glaisdale, 'The Renton Report - Ten Years On', *Statute Law Review*, 1985

*Joseph Kimble, 'Plain English: A Charter for Clear Writing', *Thomas M Cooley Law Review (Michigan, USA)*, Vol 9:1,1992

Richard Lanham, *Revising Prose*, Charles Scribner, 1979

*Law Reform Commission of Victoria, *Plain English and the Law: Report*, 1987

*Law Reform Commission of Victoria, *Plain English and the Law: Drafting Manual (Appendix 1), 1987*.

*David Mellinkoff, *The Language of the Law*, Little, Brown and Company, 1963

*David Mellinkoff, *Legal Writing: Sense and Nonsense*,
West Publishing Company, 1982

Plain English Campaign, *The Plain English Story*, 1993 (3rd
Edition)

*Steven Stark, *'Why Lawyers can't write,'* Harvard Law
Review, Vol 97, 1984

*Richard Thomas, *Plain words for Consumers: The Language
and Layout of Consumer Contracts: The case for a Plain
Language Law*, National Consumer Council, 1984

*Richard Thomas, *Plain Language for Lawyers*, National
Consumer Council, 1984

*Richard Wydick, *Plain English for Lawyers*, Carolina
Academic Press, 1985.